This journal belongs to

For God says, "At just the right time, I heard you.
On the day of salvation, I helped you." Indeed, God is ready
to help you right now. Today is the day of salvation.

2 CORINTHIANS 6:2 NLT

God has made everything that is right, true, loving, and good available to you through His Son, Jesus Christ. It is called salvation. Salvation means victory and deliverance from the pain and judgment of sin; freedom from the bondage of Satan and the powers of darkness; and peace, joy, and fellowship with God. Because of His salvation, you can have your best day every day!

It is my hope and prayer that God will use this journal to bless and enrich your life.

~ Roy Lessin

Today Is Your Best Day

ROY LESSIN

Ellie
Claire™

gift & paper expressions

...inspired by life

TODAY IS YOUR BEST DAY BECAUSE OF...

Salvation

This is the day which the LORD hath made;
we will rejoice and be glad in it.

PSALM 118:24 KJV

Salvation means that God has not said to you, "I want you to work your way to Me. I want you to try to save yourself by being good." Instead, God has said to you, "You don't have to work your way to Me, because I have come to you. I sent My Son to earth to die for you, be buried for you, and rise from the dead for you. He shed His blood on the cross so that your sins can be forgiven."

Salvation is God's free gift to you because of His grace and mercy. You cannot earn it. Salvation can only be received by faith alone in Jesus Christ.

Salvation also brings you the hope of eternal life. Salvation means that you will not be lost, or have to pay the penalty for your sins, because Jesus has paid that penalty by dying in your place. It means that you have escaped eternal condemnation and separation from God, and will have a home with Him in heaven forever.

Today Is Your Best Day Because...

You Are Here

In God we boast all day long, and praise Your name forever.

PSALM 44:8 NKJV

If you are in Jesus Christ and your heart is committed to God's plan for your life, it means that today is your best day. It is not your best day because everything is going perfectly, or because you are living in ideal circumstances. It is not your best day because you are in optimum health, or because everything is going your way.

Today is your best day because you are here. God has placed you in this moment of time for a purpose, and the things that happen to you today will be an unfolding of that purpose. What happened to you yesterday, however easy or difficult, was used by God to help prepare you for what He has for you today. God will use what happens today to prepare you for what He has for you in future days. God has used your past and worked it all together for the good, and He will use this day to add to the good that He has already worked on your behalf.

Today Is Your Best Day Because…

You Can Grow in His Love

*The steps of a good man are ordered by the L ORD,
and He delights in his way.*

P SALM 37:23 NKJV

Today is your best day because you can grow a little more in your faith,
in your maturity, and in your intimacy with Jesus. Today you can take
another step deeper as you grow in His love, another step farther as you
obediently walk with Him. Today is your best day because it has brought
you one day closer to the coming of the Lord.

You may be going through a very difficult time today, but that does
not mean this is your worst day. God will use the difficulty to produce
precious things within you that you will treasure in days to come. There
may be pressures in your day, but God uses pressure to form diamonds.
There may be a fiery trial in your day, but God uses fire to purify gold.
There may an irritant in your day, but God uses irritants to create pearls.
If you are in need of comfort today, God will bring His comfort to you,
and the comfort you receive will help you comfort someone tomorrow.

Today Is Your Best Day Because of...

Faith

For therein is the righteousness of God revealed from faith to faith:
as it is written, The just shall live by faith.

ROMANS 1:17 KJV

There are two ways that we can walk through a day. One is to walk by sight and the other is to walk by faith. To walk by sight means to allow the "reality" around us to impact our thoughts, our motivation, and our emotions. To walk by faith means to walk in a different kind of reality. The Bible tells us that there are two realities: one that is seen, the other that is unseen. There are two realities because there are two worlds, one physical and the other spiritual.

As you walk through this day in both worlds, God wants you to live by faith and not by sight. Faith sees what your physical eyes can   never see, knows what your natural mind can never comprehend, and possesses what your physical arms can never hold. Faith says "yes" to everything God declares to be true, stands upon everything God says is certain, and counts upon everything God says will come to pass.

All Things Are Possible

What is faith? It is the confident assurance that what we hope for is going to happen. It is the evidence of things we cannot yet see. So, you see, it is impossible to please God without faith. Anyone who wants to come to him must believe that there is a God and that he rewards those who sincerely seek him.

HEBREWS 11:1, 6 NLT

Your faith in God today is your lifeline to His heartbeat. Faith is the hand that reaches up and takes hold of God's promises and gathers in the spiritual treasures that are found in Christ. Faith sees the sunshine of God's face, even when there are dark clouds all around.

What things are possible for you today through faith? All things are possible, because your faith is in the God who knows no impossibilities. When the things that you are experiencing don't make sense, faith says, "God knows what He is doing." When you are fearful to take the next step, faith says, "God will not fail me."

Where will your faith journey with God lead you today? Whatever the step may be, wherever the path may lead, you can be certain that your obedience of faith will always bring you into His best.

Today Is Your Best Day Because of...

Jesus' Name

Wherefore God also hath highly exalted him, and given him
a name which is above every name:
That at the name of Jesus every knee should bow, of things in heaven,
and things in earth, and things under the earth.

PHILIPPIANS 2:9–10 KJV

Jesus' name is above every name. His name is so great that the Bible gives Him many other names to help us understand how mighty He truly is. As you go through this day, consider His glorious names and the impact they have upon your life.

He is Alpha and Omega, the first and final word in every issue that concerns you. As the Bread of Life He nurtures and sustains you. As your Captain He is charting your course and guiding your rudder. He is the Chief Shepherd, leading you to still waters and quiet resting places. He is your Deliverer, setting you free from the bondage of sin. He is the Beloved, bringing you the Father's heart. He is Jesus the Lamb of God, your Savior and sacrifice. He is your Refuge and your eternal hope.

TODAY IS YOUR BEST DAY BECAUSE…

You Are in Christ

God alone made it possible for you to be in Christ Jesus.
For our benefit God made Christ to be wisdom itself. He is the one
who made us acceptable to God. He made us pure and holy,
and he gave himself to purchase our freedom.

1 CORINTHIANS 1:30 NLT

As a child of God, today is your best day because you are in Christ. Your best day is not founded in what you've accomplished, but in who you are in Christ.

Because you are *in* Christ, everything that is true about Christ will have an impact upon you. As you go through this day, consider all that is yours because you are in Christ. You stand before God with your past forgiven and forgotten. You travel on paths of victory as you walk with your hand in His. You have a new calling, a new purpose, and a new direction, and your life is under His ownership and watch-care. Showered with grace and kindness, you have a relationship with Jesus that will never end. You are God's masterpiece in the making, and you can go through this day clothed with the righteousness of Christ.

TODAY IS YOUR BEST DAY BECAUSE...

Christ Is in You

*For it has pleased God to tell his people that the riches and glory of
Christ are for you Gentiles, too. For this is the secret: Christ lives
in you, and this is your assurance that you will share in his glory.*

COLOSSIANS 1:27 NLT

One of the glorious things about the Christian life is that God not only
places you in Christ, but Christ also comes to live in you. Being in Christ
means that you receive the benefits of all that He has done for you, and
Christ in you means that you receive the benefits of His presence,
character, and nature within you.

Your position before God is changed when you are in Christ, and the
inward condition of your heart changes when Christ is in you. Being in
Christ brings you into heavenly realities, and Christ in you brings heavenly realities into your earthly walk. Your eyes are opened to the beauty
of God's love when you are in Christ, and Christ in you floods your heart
with that same love. When you are in Christ you see what God wants
you to become, and you can become what God wants you to be when
Christ is in you.

Christ Is Living His Life in You

Abide in Me, and I in you. As the branch cannot bear fruit of itself, unless it abides in the vine, neither can you, unless you abide in Me.

JOHN 15:4 NKJV

Christ in you means that He does the work of conforming you to His image, that He is the Master Craftsman who is shaping your life, and that He is the True Vine who is producing the good fruit of eternal life within you. Christ in you means that His strength is your strength, His peace is your peace, His power is your power, and His victory is your victory.

God is not asking you to act like Jesus today. He is asking you to surrender to Jesus and trust Him completely to be your life today. Letting Jesus be Jesus in you and through you makes this your best day.

Think of this one truth as you go through this day: everything that is good, wise, loving, righteous, true, wonderful, kind, and caring is in Jesus Christ, and Jesus Christ is living His life in me.

Your Heavenly Calling

*I strain to reach the end of the race and receive the prize
for which God, through Christ Jesus, is calling us up to heaven.*

PHILIPPIANS 3:14 NLT

The apostle Paul was a remarkable man with an amazing focus on where he was and where he was going. There was nothing Paul faced that prevented him from daily moving onward toward his heavenly calling in Christ. Problems didn't deter him, trials didn't discourage him, persecution didn't defeat him, hardships didn't weigh him down. Paul wasn't looking back or going back to anything in his past. He didn't sit around counting the miles he had traveled or the distance he had come, but he pressed forward with his eyes on the summit of God's call and the glorious view of the heavenly things that awaited him.

There is a heavenly call of God upon you today to move on and press on toward all that He has prepared for you. Yesterday's progress is all behind you. Your best day is today, and whether you take a small step forward or a giant leap, this day will move you closer than you have ever been before.

TODAY IS YOUR BEST DAY BECAUSE OF...

Mercy, Peace, and Love

May you receive more and more of God's mercy, peace, and love.

JUDE 1:2 NLT

Because of God's mercies, you can follow Him with all of your heart today. You can take each step today with a quiet heart knowing that His peace keeps you steady and His love keeps you close to His heart. His mercies declare that you are covered in His compassion, His peace proclaims that you are renewed in His rest, and His love heralds that you are bathed in His blessings of joy.

Are you tired or weary today? Allow God to renew you with His strength. When you are discouraged or downhearted, let God lift you with His love. If you are carrying a burden of sin, God's mercies can restore you. Are you in need of reassurance? Allow God to hold you in His embrace. And when you need healing, let God mend you with His touch.

Today you are His child and He is your Father—you belong to Him and He belongs to you. Today there is mercy, peace, and love for your faith to receive.

TODAY IS YOUR BEST DAY BECAUSE OF…

the Reign of Christ in Your Life

For the Kingdom of God is not just fancy talk;
it is living by God's power.

1 CORINTHIANS 4:20 NLT

The kingdom of God makes all the difference in you and in your day because you are a part of it. There is no kingdom, rule, or authority that is greater than God's kingdom. The kingdom of God is all about the reign of Jesus Christ in your life. Every benefit of the kingdom is yours because you have the King ruling your life.

Jesus reigns and rules over everything He has destroyed, over everything He has defeated, and over everything He has conquered. He is the triumphant King, the mighty Warrior, and the risen Lord. He faced the onslaughts of Satan's attacks and crushed them; He faced the temptations of sin and overcame them; He faced the grip of death and triumphed over it. Today Jesus is your authority over the kingdom of darkness, He is your deliverer over the power of sin, and He is your victory over the fear of death.

TODAY IS YOUR BEST DAY BECAUSE OF...

the Kingdom of God

But seek first the kingdom of God and His righteousness,
and all these things shall be added to you.

MATTHEW 6:33 NKJV

Jesus' kingdom within you is unshakable, indestructible, and impenetrable. Nothing can come against it and prevail. The kingdom of God means that you do not have to live this day in your own strength or your own abilities, but by Jesus' power and in Jesus' endless resources. If you are facing temptation today, resist it and let Jesus' victory be yours. If the enemy is trying to pull you down and discourage you, let Jesus' strength lift you up and cause you to stand firm. If you are facing fear or worry, let Jesus' peace be your confidence, hope, and security.

The kingdom of God is a kingdom of limitless power, ceaseless joy, and unending peace. It is a kingdom of righteousness, love, and right relationships. As you go through this day, make every decision based upon what is best for the Kingdom, because what is best for the Kingdom is also what is best for you.

Today Is Your Best Day Because...
You Are Called to Serve

*So, my dear brothers and sisters, be strong and steady,
always enthusiastic about the Lord's work, for you know
that nothing you do for the Lord is ever useless.*

1 CORINTHIANS 15:58 NLT

God has given you the grace to know Him, the strength to obey Him, and the opportunity to serve Him in all you do today. There are certain things that are important for your heart to affirm as you continue your daily walk with Jesus. You have an enemy that you must resist. Satan will use all his wiles to move your eyes away from Jesus or make your feet wander off the path that God has called you to follow. Stand fast in the victory that you have in Jesus Christ, and resist everything that is against God's will for you today.

You have a call that is certain. You are where you are and doing what you are doing because it is part of God's purpose for your life. You also have a God who will not fail. He has called you to trust in Him, live in Him, and follow Him. All that Jesus does in you and through you will make this your best day.

Today Is Your Best Day Because...

You Serve the Lord

Serve the LORD with gladness:
come before his presence with singing.

PSALM 100:2 KJV

Today you have the awesome opportunity to serve the Lord. As God's servant you are in His hands as He transforms you into His image. In His hands, your life is the voice that speaks His words to those who need to know the truth, the hand that extends His love to those who are hurting, and the example that demonstrates His kingdom to those who need to know the way. Today you have been given the awesome privilege of being used by Him and living for Him as you serve Him in your God-given place.

Today you are the bondservant of the righteous Master, the ambassador of the great King, and the messenger of the eternal Word. As His servant, you live for His approval, look for His smile, and labor for His glory. Your eyes are fixed upon His face, your heart is fixed upon His will, your ears are fixed upon His voice, and your life is fixed upon His pleasure. All that you do, you do for love's sake.

Today Is Your Best Day Because of...

Truth

However, when He, the Spirit of truth, has come,
He will guide you into all truth; for He will not speak
on His own authority, but whatever He hears He will speak;
and He will tell you things to come.

John 16:13 NKJV

The Truth has come to deliver you, heal you, and revive you. Truth is the burning lamp that guides your feet on your pilgrim's journey, the plumb line of righteousness that directs your obedience, the foundation of your faith, and the road map that leads you through the gates of salvation.

Truth is the light of God that overcomes the darkness of every lie that seeks to rob you of your peace, steal your joy, and quench your faith. When the lie says, "God is not interested in you," the Truth says, "Cast all your cares upon Me, for I care for you." When the lie says, "God is against you," the Truth says, "Because God is for you, no one can be against you." When the lie says, "How could God love someone like you?" the Truth says, "God loves you with an everlasting love."

Today is your best day as you embrace the Truth.

TODAY IS YOUR BEST DAY BECAUSE OF...

Humility

Be submissive to one another, and be clothed with humility,
for "God resists the proud, but gives grace to the humble."

1 PETER 5:5 NKJV

Jesus, in His humility, left His exalted place in heaven and came to a lowly place on earth. He didn't seek out a place above men or equal to men. Instead, He took the place below others and became the servant of all.

Jesus' humility led Him to the lowest place of all—the cross. But through His humility God raised Him up, exalted Him to the highest place, and gave Him a name that is above all names.

Today, as your heart seeks the lowly place, humility will move you toward everything that is good and away from everything that is evil. It allows you to see your insufficiency and embrace God's adequacy. It is the place of freedom where your spirit soars, your love is perfected, and God's richest blessings abound. As your heart is yielded to the Lord in humility, the river of the Holy Spirit will fill you to overflowing with peace, and flow out through you to bless the lives of others.

TODAY IS YOUR BEST DAY BECAUSE...

You Depend on Him

*Therefore humble yourselves under the mighty hand of God,
that He may exalt you in due time.*

1 PETER 5:6 NKJV

Today is your best day because God wants you to live each moment totally and completely dependent upon Him. The response of humility in your heart affirms that Jesus is all you need, that He is more than sufficient, that He is altogether faithful, and that He will never fail you in any way through every circumstance of life.

Humility is not measured by what you do or don't do. It is not measured by what you say or how you look. Humility is measured by the attitude and disposition of your heart. It is measured by your surrender, your obedience, your faith, and your complete dependency upon God.

There are no limits to what God can do through the person who is free from pride and who, in humility, trusts in God alone, receives from God alone, and responds to God alone. Today let your heart say, "Lord, I love being nothing, so that You can be my all in all."

TODAY IS YOUR BEST DAY BECAUSE...

God Is Your All

*Now when all things are made subject to Him,
then the Son Himself will also be subject to Him who put
all things under Him, that God may be all in all.*

1 CORINTHIANS 15:28 NKJV

God fills all, sustains all, and has a purpose for all He has created. Through His promises He wants to bless your life as you trust and obey Him.

He is your shield and He will protect you. He listens to all you say in prayer. Leading you with unfailing love, He will fulfill all that He has purposed for your life. He forgives all your sins and will delight you with His presence. He will do everything that is right, leaving you in awe. He knows you completely and understands you perfectly, and He will never give you unwise counsel. He is always worthy of your praise. He will free you from all your fears and save you out of all your troubles. He is good to you, lifting you up and upholding you and protecting you, and He can be trusted at all times.

Abundantly pouring out His mercy over you, He is someone you can rejoice in, be glad in, and celebrate today.

Today Is Your Best Day Because of...

God's Plan

*"For I know the plans I have for you," declares the LORD,
"plans to prosper you and not to harm you,
plans to give you hope and a future."*

JEREMIAH 29:11 NIV

God has a plan for your life. It is a plan that will bring Him the greatest glory and make you into all He desires you to be. Today is your best day because God is working out that plan.

God's plan may not take you in the direction you were expecting. If your life were like a painting, the strokes that are being added to the canvas today may not make much sense when viewed alone. However, God doesn't waste any strokes when He uses His divine brush, for He sees the final picture and knows exactly how each stroke will fit into the painting's finished image. You may think the color being used today is too gray and needs more brilliance, but the time will come when you will see that the painting would not be complete, and the meaning of the painting would be weakened, if the gray strokes were not included in the exact places they appear.

TODAY IS YOUR BEST DAY BECAUSE...

You Can Trust God's Plan

I will bring the blind by a way they did not know;
I will lead them in paths they have not known.
I will make darkness light before them, and crooked places straight.
These things I will do for them, and not forsake them.

ISAIAH 42:16 NKJV

God's plan may not take you in the direction you were expecting, it may not fit into your natural way of reasoning, and it may even seem to contradict what God has promised you. Abraham had a promise from God that his son Isaac would be heir to God's covenant, but Abraham never thought that God would test his faith by asking him to offer Isaac on an altar. Joseph and Mary had no plans of traveling to Bethlehem in the late stages of Mary's pregnancy, but a Roman census forced them to the very place where the prophet declared Jesus would be born.

As you follow God's plan for your life, you do so by faith. He is not going to bring you in as a consultant to help Him decide what is best for your life. God has not called you to question Him, but to trust Him and to take the next step of obedience according to His will.

God's Wisdom

*O LORD, how manifold are thy works! in wisdom hast thou
made them all: the earth is full of thy riches.*

PSALM 104:24 KJV

God is wise. Everything He does for you, every decision He makes
on your behalf is done in wisdom. God has perfect wisdom, which
means that it is impossible for Him to make a mistake and that He
never needs to redo or undo something He has done. He never takes a
chance or makes a guess. His wisdom is complete, and He never gains
wisdom or grows in wisdom because He has all wisdom.

God's wisdom also means that He works in very practical ways in
your life. He is your wise mentor, your practical helper, and your
patient instructor. If your life were like a house, it would be built by
a master builder; if it were like a business, it would be run under the
guidance of perfect management; if it were like a tapestry, not a stitch
would be misplaced or forgotten.

Today is your best day because God's wisdom is your portion, and
He is skillfully working things out according to His own will.

Today Is Your Best Day Because of...

God's Knowledge

Then shalt thou understand the fear of the Lord, and find
the knowledge of God. For the Lord giveth wisdom:
out of his mouth cometh knowledge and understanding.

Proverbs 2:5–6 KJV

God's knowledge means that God knows. What does God know? God knows everything about all things. He knows everything there is to know about you: when you get up and when you lie down, and your actions, thoughts, and motivations. He even knows every hair on your head. God knows all about your past, all about your present, and all about your future.

God's knowledge means that God foresees. Because God foresees, He is your perfect provider. God can make provision for your needs today because His knowledge allows Him to see your need before it happens. He saw yesterday the need that you have discovered today. No need that you face today has taken God by surprise. He doesn't wait for you to have a need before He comes up with a plan to solve it. His solution was made long before you discovered you had a need.

Today Is Your Best Day Because of...

God's Presence

*He said, "My Presence will go with you, and I will give you rest."
Then he said to Him, "If Your Presence does not go with us,
do not bring us up from here."*

EXODUS 33:14–15 NKJV

There is something better than having what is best, and that is having the One who is the best. God is the best Person you can ever know, the best Friend you can ever trust, and the best Companion you can ever have. God gives you what is best because He is the best.

God gives the best kind of peace. Jesus said that He would give you His peace. The world's peace is fragile, but God's peace can withstand any storm and difficulty of life. His peace brings the glorious assurance that all is well because you are His and He is yours.

God gives the best kind of joy. Jesus said He wanted our joy to be full. The world can give only momentary happiness based upon momentary pleasures, but God gives fullness of joy, a joy that runs deeper than any circumstance of life.

Peace and joy are yours today because God's presence is yours.

Today Is Your Best Day Because of...
God's Heart of Love

I have loved you with an everlasting love;
Therefore with lovingkindness I have drawn you.

JEREMIAH 31:3 NKJV

God never says, "Give me a reason to love you." God loves you with a perfect love. He doesn't need a reason to love you because He is love, and He loves you with an everlasting love. Today His heart of love calls out for you to love Him with all of your heart.

He loves you with a perfect love. His perfect love can desire only what is the highest, the greatest, and the absolute best for your life. God commands you to love Him because He is the highest choice and the greatest good that you could ever choose. He could never say to you, "Love people more than Me; love doing good more than Me; love life more than Me." All of these things, as good as they are in themselves, can be enemies of the best when they are in the wrong place in our lives.

God gives the best kind of love. His love is unconditional.

Today Is Your Best Day Because...

You Can Give His Love Away

Now hope does not disappoint, because the love of God has been poured out in our hearts by the Holy Spirit who was given to us.

ROMANS 5:5 NKJV

God is love, and His love is the best kind of love you can have in your heart. The beautiful thing about God's love is that it is a giving love—a love that flows in abundance with kindness, generosity, and goodness. It is a love that restores, mends, and heals.

The love that God has poured into you is also the love that He wants to pour out through you. Today is your best day because you have the awesome privilege to give His love away to other people.

Be sensitive to the Holy Spirit's leading of love in your life today. Count on His love, lean on His love, and draw on His love to be the source of God's love through you. It may be expressed through a prayer you offer, through a word you speak, through an embrace you extend, through a kindness you perform, or even through a smile you give.

Today Is Your Best Day Because of...

God's Timing

My times are in Your hand.

PSALM 31:15 NKJV

Like a train, your life has a starting point and a final destination. God, like a skilled engineer and the owner of the line, is the One who makes your schedule and keeps everything running on His timetable. He knows when you need to leave a station in life and when you need to arrive at the next one. Along the way He brings people in and out of your life so that you can minister to them and they can minister to you. God is also in your stops and starts, and although your journey may sometimes seem slow, God knows exactly where you are and what He is doing.

Today is your best day because you are exactly where God wants you to be on this phase of your journey. It may be that you are waiting for Him to fulfill His promise to you, or you are anxious to move into something new, but God wants you to wait on Him until He is ready to fulfill what He has promised. Today the important thing to remember is that the best place to be is exactly where God has you at this moment.

TODAY IS YOUR BEST DAY BECAUSE OF...

the Blood of Jesus

You were not redeemed with corruptible things,
like silver or gold, from your aimless conduct received by tradition
from your fathers, but with the precious blood of Christ,
as of a lamb without blemish and without spot.

1 PETER 1:18–19 NKJV

How greatly blessed you are today because of the blood of Jesus Christ. Without His precious blood your day would be covered in darkness and despair; instead, your day is flooded with light and enriched with every spiritual blessing. The blood of Jesus has delivered you from the cruelty of a harsh taskmaster and brought you into the tender care of a loving Father.

The blood of Jesus cleanses you from the stain of sin and looses you from the chains of sin. It restores and reconciles you to God.

Why is today your best day? It is your best day because the blood of Jesus has not lost its power (and will *never* lose its power) to make it possible for you to begin this day forgiven, to be clothed in garments of righteousness, and to face the day with clean hands and a pure heart.

Redemption

Neither by the blood of goats and calves,
but by [Jesus'] own blood he entered in once into the holy place,
having obtained eternal redemption for us.

HEBREWS 9:12 KJV

Jesus Christ is your Redeemer, and His shed blood has secured your redemption. The Bible tells us that we were all prisoners who were held captive, without the hope of freedom, unless a ransom price was paid to free us. The blood of Jesus Christ is the ransom price that was paid to set us free from the captivity of Satan and the enslavement of sin.

When the Bible says that you have been redeemed, it means that you have been absolutely freed from all that had you bound in the past. Redemption also means that you have been redeemed from the guilt and condemnation that sin had over you.

Today is your best day because God was willing to pay the price of the death of His Son to redeem you as His own. He has redeemed you because He loves you and has a plan and purpose for your life.

Today Is Your Best Day Because...

Jesus Is 100 Percent

This High Priest of ours understands our weaknesses, for he faced all of the same temptations we do, yet he did not sin.

Hebrews 4:15 nlt

Even though everything around you is flawed and imperfect, today is your best day because you have Jesus. Jesus is 100 percent perfect in all His ways, in all He is, and in all He does. His Father sent Him here as the spotless Lamb of God who would offer Himself upon the cross as a sacrifice for your sins. Jesus fully obeyed His Father, and through His perfect obedience He glorified the Father.

In His nature and character, Jesus is without fault or flaw. He is completely faithful. He will never fail you. Every promise He has made is true; there is not one lie or exaggeration in anything that He has ever said. Today Jesus is your 100 percent Savior.

Jesus did not let you down when He lived on earth, when He died on the cross, when He rose from the dead, or when He was seated at the right hand of the Father, and He will not let you down today.

TODAY IS YOUR BEST DAY BECAUSE OF…

God's True Joy

And the ransomed of the LORD shall return, and come to Zion with songs and everlasting joy upon their heads: they shall obtain joy and gladness, and sorrow and sighing shall flee away.

ISAIAH 35:10 KJV

Joy is one of the great benefits of the kingdom of God within your life. It is the melody of heaven that is placed in your heart, the Holy Spirit's symphony that is played within your spirit, and the theme song of every person who trusts in the Lord and knows His love.

Joy is the highest level of delight that a person can experience. Human happiness is dependent upon the experiences and circumstances of life, while joy is dependent upon God alone. God, not your personality type, is the source of your joy.

It is easy to think that joy can come from other things apart from God, but there is no lasting satisfaction in any material thing that we possess. They can never replace the true joys that come to us from God alone. Today joy flows from His heart to yours like a fountain that will never run dry.

the Fullness of Joy

The joy of the LORD is your strength.

NEHEMIAH 8:10 NKJV

Joy is like energy that flows through you to lighten your load, renew your zeal, and quicken your steps. It is the strength in your legs that helps you stand firm and steady in times of trial, the power in your arms that enables you to hold on to God's promises, and the rejoicing in your voice that speaks forth the victory of the Lord over every area of your life.

God not only wants you to have His joy reigning in your heart today, but He wants your joy to become great joy, and He wants great joy to become the fullness of joy. God wants you to be immersed in the delights of His joy today so that every fiber of your being is filled with rejoicing and celebration of His goodness.

We move into the highest levels of joy when we abide in the love of the Father, and through Him, reach out to love others. Today is your best day when you walk in the fullness of His joy, and as you allow the Father to fill you with His love and love others through you.

TODAY IS YOUR BEST DAY BECAUSE OF...

Peace

Now the Lord of peace himself give you peace always by all means.
The Lord be with you all.

2 THESSALONIANS 3:16 KJV

Peace has been defined in many ways—calm in the midst of a storm, quiet in the midst of turmoil, tranquility in the midst of uncertainty. The presence of peace is the absence of confusion and strife. Peace can also be defined as the deep and unshakable conviction that all is well with your soul. It comes when your heart is confident that God is in control, not only of the universe, but of your life as well. Peace also comes by knowing that God is for you and by being in harmony with God as you live from day to day.

Peace is also the *shalom* of God. One of God's names is Jehovah-Shalom. It means that God not only gives peace, but He *is* peace. Shalom is a word that embraces God's favor, blessing, prosperity, health, rest, wholeness, and friendship.

Today is your best day because the God of peace and the peace of God are your portion—a peace that no circumstance, thing, or person can either increase or diminish.

Today Is Your Best Day Because...

Grace Is Freely Given

For by grace you have been saved through faith,
and that not of yourselves; it is the gift of God.

EPHESIANS 2:8 NKJV

Grace makes it possible for today to be your best day. It demands nothing and gives everything God desires you to have. Through grace, God has pulled out all the stops and poured His abundant favor upon you in Jesus Christ. Grace points you to Jesus and says, "All that is His is freely yours. All mercy, all blessings, all strength, all righteousness, all kindness are yours today in Jesus Christ."

Whenever the word *grace* appears in the Scriptures, there is another word that often appears nearby. That word is *given*. God has showered you with grace without any expectation of return. You do not need to earn something that you have already been given. Even when you need more grace, God supplies it freely. How did you receive grace in the first place? God extended His grace to you while you were a sinner. He did not extend His grace to you because you were religious or full of good works. His grace came to you through the cross. He extended His grace to you based upon what His Son did for you.

TODAY IS YOUR BEST DAY BECAUSE OF...

the Blessings of Grace

But God, who is rich in mercy, because of His great love with which
He loved us, even when we were dead in trespasses,
made us alive together with Christ (by grace you have been saved)...
that in the ages to come He might show the exceeding riches
of His grace in His kindness toward us in Christ Jesus.

EPHESIANS 2:4–7 NKJV

God extends grace to you today. Nothing that you have done as a believer in Christ has earned you more grace. Bible reading, prayer, giving, and Christian service don't mean that you have earned the right to have more grace poured out upon you. If it did, grace would not be grace. You will never find the word *deserved* associated with grace.

Every joy that fills your heart and every delight that satisfies your soul are yours today because of the benefits of grace. Grace does not hang something over your head and say, "You owe Me and I expect you to pay Me back." Grace is the absolute free expression of God's loving heart. The motivation of grace is to bountifully bless you.

TODAY IS YOUR BEST DAY BECAUSE OF...

the Benefits of Grace

Who hath saved us, and called us with an holy calling,
not according to our works, but according to his own purpose and grace,
which was given us in Christ Jesus before the world began.

2 TIMOTHY 1:9 KJV

There are so many benefits of grace that are yours today. Your forgiveness of sin, your justification before God, your redemption from the slavery of sin, your deliverance from evil, and your future home in heaven are yours today because of grace.

Grace enables you to do all God calls you to do today. Success is not based today upon what you can accomplish, but upon what He will do through you. Grace is not about your strength, but about His mighty power working in you, even in the time of your greatest weakness.

Grace builds you up, lifts you up, and keeps you standing. Grace is heard in the sound of God's voice speaking over and over into your ear, "I am for you today. I am with you today. I am the source of everything good, everything lovely, everything holy, and everything mighty."

the Assurance of Grace

But where sin abounded, grace did much more abound.

ROMANS 5:20 KJV

Grace assures you of a glorious future and an overwhelming inheritance that is yours in Jesus Christ. You are victorious today because Jesus is the triumphant One. You are more than a conqueror because He has conquered all. You reign in life because He reigns.

Where sin once abounded, grace abounds even more. Where darkness ruled, grace overruled. Grace is never poured out to you like raindrops, but like a cascading waterfall. Grace is never a license to sin or a cloak for sin. Grace brings us into a life that is greater than what sin could ever offer us. Grace extends the hand that lifts us out of the miry clay.

Gifts that come to you from God are grace gifts. His grace gifts to you will be different from the grace gifts He gives to others. Grace does not play favorites. The gifts that have been given to you from God are the perfect gifts that are needed for you to fulfill His will and His calling in your life.

Today Is Your Best Day Because of…
the Abundance of Grace

And God is able to make all grace abound toward you;
that ye, always having all sufficiency in all things,
may abound to every good work.

2 Corinthians 9:8 kjv

Grace abounds to you today with so many favors, blessings, and joys. Without His grace we were songbirds without a song, but by His grace we have been given a new song to sing and a melody of praise for our hearts to rejoice in. We were trees bearing bitter fruit, but now by His grace we bear sweet, lush fruit that remains.

Without His grace our heads hung low and turned away from the light of His love; by His grace our heads have been lifted up, and our hearts have been flooded with His glorious light. We were defenseless against the attacks of the enemy, but by His grace we now stand against the enemy triumphantly.

Without His grace we lived in confusion, were lost, and had no clear direction; but by His grace we have been found, and His wisdom guides our lives as He makes straight paths for our feet.

the Sufficiency of Grace

He said to me, "My grace is sufficient for you, for My strength is made perfect in weakness." Therefore most gladly I will rather boast in my infirmities, that the power of Christ may rest upon me....
For when I am weak, then I am strong.

2 CORINTHIANS 12:9–10 NKJV

Without His grace we were blind, stumbling about in the darkness; but now by His grace our purpose has been made known, and we daily walk in the good things that He has prepared for us.

We were fearful, motivated by self-interests, and striving to succeed. Now by His grace we have entered into His rest, walk in His peace, and daily live for His glory.

Without His grace we were without hope or the assurance of heaven, and bound by the fear of death; but by His grace we abound in hope, rejoice in the certainty of the resurrection, and glory in knowing that the very best is still ahead.

TODAY IS YOUR BEST DAY BECAUSE...

Jesus Sent the Holy Spirit

Nevertheless I tell you the truth; It is expedient for you that I go away:
for if I go not away, the Comforter will not come unto you;
but if I depart, I will send him unto you.

JOHN 16:7 KJV

Today is your best day because Jesus sent the Holy Spirit. The Holy Spirit is our divine companion, our comforter, and the one who has come alongside us. How blessed we are to have the Holy Spirit within our lives, abiding with us, speaking to us, and walking with us as we go through our day.

The Holy Spirit is truer than the truest friend. Every pleasing quality of a close and tender friend is found in the Holy Spirit. He knows everything about you, loves you without reservation or condition, cares about every need you face, and will never betray your trust. The Holy Spirit is completely dependable and fully available.

Jesus sent the Holy Spirit, not to be with you partially so you could have a little taste of His presence, but to be in your life in fullness. Jesus wants you to be submerged in, clothed with, and empowered by the Holy Spirit.

the Work of the Holy Spirit

The Helper, the Holy Spirit, whom the Father will send in My name,
He will teach you all things, and bring to your remembrance
all things that I said to you.

JOHN 14:26 NKJV

The Holy Spirit has been sent to take you deeper into the love of God. Compare this to deep-sea diving: The ocean is a great expanse, and its depths are just beginning to be explored in new ways. Modern technology and engineering have created machines that can carry man to depths never before thought possible. Similarly, the Holy Spirit can take you into the depths of God's love that you've never seen, known, or understood before.

The Holy Spirit has also been sent to take you higher and allow your eyes to see more of the greatness and glory of God's majesty. Through the space program, man has been able to explore new heights, seeing things and doing things that were thought impossible a century ago. The Holy Spirit can cause your spirit to ascend into the heights of God's glory, to behold the beauty of the Lord, and to celebrate His majesty with a heart that is in awe of His splendor.

Today Is Your Best Day Because of…

the Purpose of the Holy Spirit

And now you also have heard the truth, the Good News that God saves you.
And when you believed in Christ, he identified you as his own by giving you
the Holy Spirit, whom he promised long ago.

EPHESIANS 1:13 NLT

The Holy Spirit is wonderful! His purpose is to bring to pass all that God has planned for you, to make real all that Jesus has done for you, and to reveal all that the Scriptures declare to you.

The Holy Spirit was involved in your life long before you put your trust in Jesus Christ. He pursued you when you walked according to your own way and wooed you to the heart of God when your heart was fixed upon other things.

The Holy Spirit points you to Jesus' life, character, and works. His encouragement is the greatest when your valleys are the deepest; His comfort is the sweetest when your burdens are the heaviest; His support is the strongest when your strength is the weakest.

Today is your best day because of the calling, gifting, and empowering of the Holy Spirit upon your life.

the Holy Spirit's Power and Protection

And straightway coming up out of the water, he saw the heavens opened, and the Spirit like a dove descending upon him.

MARK 1:10 KJV

The Holy Spirit is likened to the wind. He can come to you as a mighty wind, bringing God's awesome power as He did at the day of Pentecost. His power will give you great boldness and fully equip you for what God has prepared for you today. He can also come to you as a gentle breeze, cooling you and delighting you with His sweet presence. Like the wind, the Holy Spirit is also the breath of God that quickens you and brings you spiritual life. The Holy Spirit is the atmosphere of heaven that your spirit breathes.

The Holy Spirit is also likened to a dove. He can come upon you in a gentle way and hover over your life as He hovered over the waters at the time of creation. This hovering is likened to a bird as she flutters over her young with her wings. Like the protective bird, the Holy Spirit guards your life and watches over the good work that God has begun in you.

Today Is Your Best Day Because...

the Holy Spirit Fills You

*Now may the God of hope fill you with all joy and peace in believing,
that you may abound in hope by the power of the Holy Spirit.*

Romans 15:13 NKJV

The Holy Spirit is likened to a river. He moves in your life in a flowing motion, directing you according to God's will and purpose for your life. The headwaters begin at the throne of God and flow out with mercy and grace. He flows deeply within you, and His sparkling clear waters brilliantly reflect the sunlight of Jesus' perfect love.

The Holy Spirit is also likened to fire. He illuminates your way and opens your understanding, causing you to see things you've never seen before. His flame is also a purifying fire that burns away the empty things in your life, leaving only those things that have an eternal value.

The Holy Spirit is likened to oil. He is the One who is poured out upon you like a healing balm—to soothe, calm, and comfort. He is the One who renews your strength and refreshes your spirit. The Holy Spirit is being poured out upon you today.

Today Is Your Best Day Because…

God Gives You His Promises

*They are the people of Israel, chosen to be God's special children.
God revealed his glory to them. He made covenants with them
and gave his law to them. They have the privilege of worshiping him
and receiving his wonderful promises.*

ROMANS 9:4 NLT

You have so much going for you today, because so much has been given to you by God. You have the fullness of His grace, the bounty of His mercies, the greatness of His power, the beauty of His presence, and the wonders of His love. You have been blessed with the fellowship of other believers, the revelation of the sacred Scriptures, the daily intercession of Jesus Christ, the watchful ministry of heavenly angels, and you have been given the precious promises spoken from the heart of God.

God's promises are completely reliable because God is completely dependable. His promises are true because He cannot lie. He has given you His promises because He wants you to know what is in His heart for you today. God's promises not only assure you that He will give you all that is best today, but that His best will also be a glorious part of your future.

TODAY IS YOUR BEST DAY BECAUSE...

You Can Receive God's Promises

*As we know Jesus better, his divine power gives us everything we
need for living a godly life.... And by that same mighty power,
he has given us all of his rich and wonderful promises.... So make
every effort to apply the benefits of these promises to your life.*

2 PETER 1:3–5 NLT

God doesn't want you to simply know *about* His promises. He wants your faith to actively reach out and *take* them as your own.

When God makes a promise to you, He never fails to keep it because He never forgets. His promise book is the Word of God, and He knows everything that is in it, down to the smallest detail.

God never fails to keep a promise He has made to you because of limited resources or because what He has promised you in Christ is no longer available. Every promise that God has made will cause you to know Him better, enjoy Him more fully, and love Him more deeply. His promises are yours today.

TODAY IS YOUR BEST DAY BECAUSE OF...
God's Character

*"But let him who glories glory in this, that he understands and knows Me,
that I am the LORD, exercising lovingkindness, judgment,
and righteousness in the earth. For in these I delight," says the LORD.*

JEREMIAH 9:24 NKJV

God's character is the foundation that you build your life upon, the rock
that your feet stand upon, and the strong tower that your faith leans
upon. God is completely dependable, unshakable, and unmovable.

What does your faith in God's character mean to you today? It means
that you know the sun still shines even though there are dark clouds
overhead, that the anchor of your soul still holds even though the storm
rages on, that your next step is certain even though a heavy fog covers
your pathway. Faith in God's character means that comfort will be your
portion even though you are facing a dark valley, that a strong hand is
holding yours even though there is nothing to hang on to as you walk
near the mountain's edge.

Today is in God's hands, and so are you. His hands are strong and they
will uphold you. Today is your best day because the One who holds you
up will never let you down!

TODAY IS YOUR BEST DAY BECAUSE OF...

God's Leading

For thou art my rock and my fortress;
therefore for thy name's sake lead me, and guide me.

PSALM 31:3 KJV

Today is your best day because God will lead you in His paths and direct your steps. Today you will take steps you have never taken before, learn things you've never known before, and have opportunities you've never been given before. God has many ways of showing you His ways and leading you in His will. Some of these include the Holy Scriptures, the voice of the Holy Spirit, the wise counsel of godly people, His provisions, and His peace within your heart.

God will lead you into new discoveries of spiritual truth, into new places of ministry, into new relationships, into new avenues of praise, into new steps of obedience, or into new ways of practically expressing His love to others.

Trust in the Lord to lead you today. He will use you in ways that you may not be aware of, or He may use you in a very clear and practical way to bless the life of someone in need.

TODAY IS YOUR BEST DAY BECAUSE OF…

Heavenly Riches

You know how full of love and kindness our Lord Jesus Christ was.
Though he was very rich, yet for your sakes he became poor,
so that by his poverty he could make you rich.

2 CORINTHIANS 8:9 NLT

Jesus Christ has truly made you rich in the things that are of the highest value. He has made His heavenly riches yours because He is rich in mercy toward you. This means that God will enrich your life, supply your needs, and satisfy your soul. He desires to nurture your spirit, build up your faith, increase your strength, fill your heart, and abundantly bless you.

Your heavenly riches will never fade, rust, or be stolen away. You are rich in grace, rich in favor, and rich in blessings. The blessings that are yours in Christ are greater than all material blessings here on earth.

Here are some of the rich blessings that are yours: You can be filled with all joy and peace, and His love fills your heart. You are freely justified and can abound in hope. You are dead to sin and alive to God. You are under grace and have a divine calling.

TODAY IS YOUR BEST DAY BECAUSE OF...

Spiritual Riches

Bless the LORD, O my soul, and forget not all His benefits.

PSALM 103:2 NKJV

God wants you to know the blessings that are yours now, so that you can benefit from them today. You are being conformed to Christ's image and have been given the mind of Christ. You are a child of God and His heir. Spiritual victory is yours. You have been redeemed and are enriched in everything. You can be strengthened by His might, and you have His wisdom, righteousness, and sanctification.

You have been given an inheritance and are comforted in hard times. Each day you can discover new things about God's love. Seated with Christ, you can be filled with God's fullness. With access to God you can always be triumphant.

You have God's power working in you, boldness in prayer, and a spiritual gifting. Complete in Him, you can be filled with the knowledge of His will. Having been delivered from darkness, you are a child of the light. You are cleansed and set apart for God's purposes, and you can prosper in body, soul, and spirit. Through His greatness you can overcome.

TODAY IS YOUR BEST DAY BECAUSE OF…

What Jesus Says

Your words were found, and I ate them, and Your word was to me the joy and rejoicing of my heart; For I am called by Your name, O LORD God of hosts.

JEREMIAH 15:16 NKJV

As in any new relationship where you love to hear positive encouragement, Jesus is saying things to you today that will make your hopes soar, increase your faith, and cause your heart to grow closer to His.

Here are some things that Jesus is saying to you today (and some of the things He isn't saying). He doesn't say, "Get away from Me." He says, "Come to Me." He doesn't say that what He has to give is not available to you. He says, "Abide in Me." He doesn't say you'll have to make it on your own. He says, "I am your Shepherd." He doesn't say He will cut you off from His blessings. He says, "Come to Me and drink." He doesn't say He cannot use you. He says, "I will make you fishers of men." He doesn't say, "Give Me a good reason to love you." He says, "I love you." He doesn't say you won't be welcome in heaven. He says, "I go to prepare a place for you."

Today Is Your Best Day Because of...

What God Says

I will hear what God the LORD will speak:
for he will speak peace unto his people, and to his saints.

PSALM 85:8 KJV

God is your Father through your personal relationship with His Son, Jesus Christ. You are God's child, and as your Father, He has many things that He wants you to know and to hold on to as treasures from Him.

Here are some of the things that His heart speaks (and doesn't speak) to your heart today. God doesn't say He has no interest in you. He says, "I care for you." He doesn't tell you not to count on Him. He says, "I will never fail you." He doesn't say that you have plenty of reasons to be fearful. He says, "Do not be afraid." He doesn't say there are things in your life that are too big for Him to handle. He says, "Trust Me." He doesn't say there are some things that are out of His control. He says, "I rule over all." He doesn't say He can't figure out what to do with you. He says, "I know the plans I have for you."

TODAY IS YOUR BEST DAY BECAUSE OF…

the Will of God

Don't copy the behavior and customs of this world, but let God
transform you into a new person by changing the way you think.
Then you will know what God wants you to do, and you will know
how good and pleasing and perfect his will really is.

ROMANS 12:2 NLT

Living in the will of God means that today is your best day. His will is perfectly suited for you. Living in His will brings you the deepest peace, the greatest joy, and the highest purpose you can know.

Being in the will of God for your life may mean difficulty, suffering, or persecution, but it will never mean that you could have chosen something better or of higher good. Living in the will of God may mean that someone will misunderstand you, disapprove of what you're doing, or oppose you. However, this is your best day because you don't have to defend yourself—God is your defender; you don't have to look out for yourself—God is your provider. Living in the will of God means that you are living under the approval of God, and His approval is all you really need.

Today Is Your Best Day Because of...
the Power of Prayer

Let us therefore come boldly unto the throne of grace, that we may obtain mercy, and find grace to help in time of need.

Hebrews 4:16 KJV

The benefits of prayer are endless, the effectiveness of prayer is limitless, and the opportunities in prayer are boundless. Today is your best day because of the impact, the influence, and the power of prayer.

Nothing can shut down prayer—no wall, no policy, and no law. Through prayer you can go places you've never been, impact people you've never met, discover things you've never known, open up your heart to joys you've never experienced, and move the hand of God in ways you've never seen.

God, through prayer, invites you to receive of His grace and mercy whenever you are in need. He encourages you to ask, to knock, and to call upon Him so that you may learn His will, know His heart, and receive His answers. Your prayers can have an important part in seeing a lost soul saved, a weak person strengthened, a needy person helped, a weary person encouraged, and a bound person set free.

Answers to Prayer

Don't worry about anything; instead, pray about everything.
Tell God what you need, and thank him for all he has done.

PHILIPPIANS 4:6 NLT

Why has God called us to prayer? Prayer allows us to discover something new and very special about God's personal love and care.

A few months after my wife and I were married, we were living in a small seacoast city in Baja California, studying the Spanish language with my brother and his wife in preparation for mission work in Mexico. One morning two fuses blew in our fuse box, leaving us without electricity. We also needed to replace our five-gallon jug of drinking water. In all, we needed forty cents. Between the four of us we had no money, but we looked to the Lord for our need.

Later my brother went for a walk on the beach. Soon he came back with a five-peso bill he had found sticking out of the sand! It was the exact amount we needed. How did God do that? None of us had an answer, but it was an affirmation of how much God loved us and faithfully took care of us. How has God creatively answered your prayers?

Today Is Your Best Day Because of…
God's Wings of Protection

The Lord repay your work, and a full reward be given you by the Lord God of Israel, under whose wings you have come for refuge.

RUTH 2:12 NKJV

God uses the term *wings* to help you understand more fully what it means to have His presence throughout your day and His covering over you moment by moment. As your covering, God's wings shield you and cast a shadow over you. His shadow is like the welcome relief provided by a shade tree on a hot summer's day. God's wings shade you from the damaging rays of adversity and from the heat of every trial and calamity. As an expression of His care, God's wings draw you close to His heart. He knows your every movement, senses your every need, hears your every cry, and feels your every heartbeat.

As an expression of His protection, God's wings shield you from the searching eye of every predator that seeks to devour or destroy you. He is your protector against every scheme of the enemy, every lie and deception, and every enticement that would try to move you away from His heart.

God's Wings of Compassion

Keep me as the apple of Your eye;
hide me under the shadow of Your wings.

PSALM 17:8 NKJV

As an expression of His strength, God's wings are an extension of His tender compassion. His purpose is to keep you healthy and strong, well fed and nurtured, vibrant and full of life. When you are weak or ill, He wraps His wings around you as a mother would wrap her child in a blanket. He assures you of His love, draws you close, keeps you warm, feeds you with the food of His faithfulness, renews your vitality, and causes you to grow strong. God's wings carry you to new heights, to new adventures of faith, to new discoveries of His majesty, and to new vistas of grace that your heart can explore and delight in.

Today you are under God's extreme watch-care. He calls you to draw near and trust fully in the covering of His wings. You are the Lord's delight and the apple of His eye. Today is your best day because your life couldn't be in better hands or under better care.

His Preparation

But now, O LORD, thou art our father; we are the clay,
and thou our potter; and we all are the work of thy hand.

ISAIAH 64:8 KJV

Like clay in the hands of a skilled craftsman, God is forming you for His purposes and molding you as a vessel fit for the Master's use. The vessel He is shaping you into will have no errors in its design. Do not think that your vessel needs to be a certain shape or size to be significant. God may shape you into a tiny vessel that can easily be used to pour oil into the wounds of others; He may shape you as a candle and place you in a dark place to shine for Him; He may shape you into a cup to bring living water to a thirsty soul; He may shape you into a handheld basin that can humbly be used to wash a disciple's feet.

God is also preparing you for what He has ahead. He is preparing you for a place, a ministry, and a people that He wants you to reach.

TODAY IS YOUR BEST DAY BECAUSE OF...

Motivation

We know how much God loves us, and we have put our trust in him.
God is love, and all who live in love live in God, and God lives
in them. And as we live in God, our love grows more perfect.

1 JOHN 4:16–17 NLT

The love God has for you and your love for Him work together to make this your best day. This relationship is possible because God loved you first. He didn't wait on you to respond to Him before He showed you His loving favor. His love pursued you when your heart was far away from His. You will never know a love as glorious and generous as the love that God has for you.

It is God's love for you that makes you a debtor of His love. Your love debt to God motivates you, not only to love Him in return, but to bring His love to others. It is Christ's love that moves you to respond to Him and to the people He brings into your life. Let all you do today flow out of the joys that come from your love relationship with Him.

TODAY IS YOUR BEST DAY BECAUSE OF...

Change

For I am about to do a brand-new thing. See, I have already begun!
Do you not see it? I will make a pathway through the wilderness for
my people to come home. I will create rivers for them in the desert!

ISAIAH 43:19 NLT

God never changes, but He is a changer. He changes darkness into light, deserts into waterways, water into wine, mountains into low places, wastelands into grain fields, death into life, ashes into beauty, mourning into joy, and rough places into smooth paths.

When God brings change it means that He is moving us out of something that has been comfortable and into something new that will cause our faith to grow, our hearts to be purified, and our vision to be broadened.

What are the heart changes God is bringing into your life? He may be bringing a new truth to your heart, allowing you to see a certain circumstance in a new way, imparting a new spiritual gift, opening up a new avenue of obedience, or setting you aside for a time of rest and refreshing. Whatever vessel God may be using, it will be the best for you and bring His very best to you.

TODAY IS YOUR BEST DAY BECAUSE OF...

Renewal

Therefore if any man be in Christ, he is a new creature:
old things are passed away; behold, all things are become new.

2 CORINTHIANS 5:17 KJV

Today is your best day because God has exchanged your old way of life for a new way of life. In Jesus, everything in your life experiences a new beginning. Your past sins no longer stand against you, and a holy life is now before you. Your new life means that the way you used to be is not the way you have to be.

Your new life is not based upon your determination but on God's transformation. It is not about following certain steps for self-improvement or making resolutions to do better. God didn't try to improve you; rather, He *renewed* you and made you a new creation in Christ. God did not take your old way of life and try to patch it up or build it up. He did something far better. He brought an end to your old way of life by crucifying it on the cross with Christ. Through the cross, God has dealt with everything in your life that was a hindrance to your relationship with Him.

Today Is Your Best Day Because of...

Newness of Life

Therefore we were buried with Him through baptism into death,
that just as Christ was raised from the dead by the glory of the Father,
even so we also should walk in newness of life.

ROMANS 6:4 NKJV

Today your old way of life has no power over you. Your new life is the life of Jesus Christ. The life of Christ in you does not need improvement. It is a resurrected life. Everything about it is good, right, freeing, and loving.

Christ's life means His power is your strength, His will is your purpose, His mind is your wisdom, His love is your motivation, and His presence is your joy. In your old way of life everything depended upon you; in your new way of life everything depends upon Christ. In your old way of life you were at the center; in your new way of life Christ is at the center. In your old way of life, you tried to be self-sufficient; in your new way of life, Christ is your sufficiency.

God's call upon you today is to walk in newness of life, and to put on your new life as you would put on a new garment.

Dependency

*Yes, I am the vine; you are the branches. Those who remain in me,
and I in them, will produce much fruit. For apart from me
you can do nothing.*

JOHN 15:5 NLT

As God's child, today is your best day because you are totally and completely dependent upon Him. There is no way that today could be your best day if you were dependent upon yourself—your finances, friends, talents, resources, looks, body, personality, mind, or emotions. Money runs out, friends come and go, talents wear down, resources diminish, and looks change. Your personality is flawed, your body is aging, your mind has limitations, and your emotions rise and fall. God is your only rock, your only security, and your only hope.

How blessed you are to be dependent upon God today. His kingdom is unshakable, His power is unquestionable, His wisdom is unmistakable, His love is undeniable. You are blessed to be dependent upon the One who is perfect, whose kingdom is without end, whose power is limitless, whose glory is endless, and whose love is boundless.

Your Life Is in His Hands

Call upon Me in the day of trouble;
I will deliver you, and you shall glorify Me.

PSALM 50:15 NKJV

Dependency upon God means that your life is in the hands of the One who created the heavens, who designed the galaxies, who painted the sunsets, who set the earth in space, and whose hand formed every creature that walks, swims, crawls, runs, or flies.

Dependency upon God means that you have set your heart upon Him and put your faith in Him. God will not fail you. When you face a problem, He will solve it; when you have a need, He will meet it; when you have a burden, He will carry it; when you face a barrier, He will help you overcome it.

Today you are as dependent upon God as your lungs are upon the air. God has made everything within you cry out to Him, and as you do, you can be sure that He will answer. Today He says, "Call to Me, and I will answer you, and show you great and mighty things, which you do not know" (Jeremiah 33:3 NKJV).

TODAY IS YOUR BEST DAY BECAUSE OF...

Jesus' Best Day

*Looking unto Jesus, the author and finisher of our faith, who for the
joy that was set before Him endured the cross, despising the shame,
and has sat downat the right hand of the throne of God.*

HEBREWS 12:2 NKJV

Was the crucifixion of Jesus Christ His worst day or His best day? From a
human perspective, everything about the cross looked like His worst day.
His beaten body, the pain of the nails being driven into His hands and
feet, the agony of hanging from beams of wood, His blood being poured
out upon the ground—all of these point to failure and defeat if we do not
understand the reason for His suffering.

From a divine perspective and a believer's perspective, the crucifixion,
with all its horror, was Jesus' *best* day. It was His best day because
prophetically this truly was the "day that the Lord had made." This was
the day the Father had planned when He sent His only begotten Son into
the world. All of Jesus' life on earth pointed to this day.

God planned Jesus' best day so that it can outshine your worst day.

TODAY IS YOUR BEST DAY BECAUSE OF...

the Cross

[He] gave Himself for us, that He might
redeem us from every lawless deed and purify for Himself
His own special people, zealous for good works.

TITUS 2:14 NKJV

The Bible tells us that Jesus endured the cross, despising its shame, for the joy that He knew would be His. It was Jesus' best day because He came to do the will of God, He would receive the reward of His suffering, He destroyed the works of the devil, He redeemed us back to God, and He glorified His Father.

Jesus' death on the cross has also made it possible for this day to be your best day. He took your sins upon Himself so that you could be forgiven, receive eternal life, be justified, have peace with God, and be His bride. His best day draws you closer to Him, to know Him, love Him, and serve Him. Through Jesus' love and suffering on that day, you can carry the hope of heaven in your heart every day.

TODAY IS YOUR BEST DAY BECAUSE OF...

Your Foundation

These words I speak to you are not mere additions to your life, homeowner improvements to your standard of living. They are foundation words, words to build a life on. If you work the words into your life, you are like a smart carpenter who dug deep and laid the foundation of his house on bedrock. When the river burst its banks and crashed against the house, nothing could shake it; it was built to last.

LUKE 6:47–48 MSG

Today is your best day because of the foundation that your life is being built upon. The Bible tells us that one day everything upon this earth will be shaken and the only things that will remain are eternal things. The only way a person's life can be secure is to build it upon Jesus and His words.

The Psalms remind us of the importance of having God as our rock and our strength. When you feel faint or feeble, God is the rock that stands higher than your emotions or inadequacies; when you are under attack from the enemy, God is your rock of defense; when you cry out to God in time of trouble, He will be your rock of deliverance.

Today Is Your Best Day Because...

You Are Saved

*Even when we were dead in sins, hath quickened us together
with Christ, (by grace ye are saved)...For by grace are ye saved
through faith; and that not of yourselves: it is the gift of God:
Not of works, lest any man should boast.*

Ephesians 2:5, 8–9 kjv

Think of it: You are saved. You are forgiven. Jesus is your Savior and your life belongs to Him. Your past sins are in the sea of God's forgetfulness. You have eternal life, you are on your way to heaven, and you have a God-given purpose here on earth.

The sky may be gray today, but you are saved; someone may have hurt you or let you down, but you are saved. You may be going through a difficult time, but you are saved. Though the enemy may be attacking you with doubts and fears, you are saved; and though you may be tired, alone, or unappreciated, you are saved.

"What we suffer now is nothing," the apostle Paul wrote, "compared to the glory he will give us later" (Romans 8:18 nlt).

Today Is Your Best Day Because…

He Will Bring You Home

I have trusted in Your mercy; my heart shall rejoice in Your salvation.
I will sing to the Lord, because He has dealt bountifully with me.

Psalm 13:5–6 NKJV

Today there is an endless number of reasons why your heart should be rejoicing and thankful that you are saved. If you weren't saved, you would be lost, under guilt and condemnation, without God and without hope in this present evil world. You would be empty inside and without peace, in bondage to the enemy, and dead in your trespasses and sins. You would have no eternal purpose and no hope of heaven. What could be worse than that?

But you are saved! Saved by God's grace, saved because God loves you, saved because He sent His only begotten Son, saved because Jesus died for you, saved because Jesus shed His blood. You are saved because God provided everything that was needed for you to come to Him and receive His loving embrace. Today you have not only been saved by Him, but you are also being kept by Him, and He will bring you safely home. What could be better than that?

Today Is Your Best Day Because...

His Righteousness Is Now Yours

Christ died for our sins, just as the Scriptures said.
He was buried, and he was raised from the dead
on the third day, just as the Scriptures said.

1 Corinthians 15:3–4 NLT

Jesus died and rose for you! Jesus' death was in the Father's heart before the world was formed. Because of God's grace and mercy toward us, we can look back over our lives at all the wrong we have done and hear our heavenly Father say to us, "You are forgiven. I have washed you clean, even whiter than snow. My Son's righteousness has become your righteousness because He died and rose for you."

When we look back over our lives at the good things we've tried to do to earn God's favor, we hear our heavenly Father say to us, "Your righteousness will never be enough to save you or keep you. No amount of work that you do can justify you in My presence. By the righteousness of the law no one can be justified. That is why My Son died and rose for you. By faith alone, His righteousness is now yours."

Jesus Died and Rose for You

Blessed be the God and Father of our Lord Jesus Christ,
who according to His abundant mercy has begotten us again to a living
hope through the resurrection of Jesus Christ from the dead.

1 PETER 1:3 NKJV

Does God love you and care about you today? Yes, Jesus died and rose for you. Does God provide for you and have a plan for your life? Does He forgive you and restore you and have a place for you in heaven? Yes, Jesus died and rose for you.

If you only knew this one truth, it would be enough. If you only had this spiritual bread to eat, it would sustain you. Jesus died and rose for you! Is this not the taproot from which the tree of life grows? Is this not the song of celebration that fills your innermost being? Is this not the source from which the healing fountains flow? Justification, sanctification, redemption, and all the other truths of Holy Scripture are yours because Jesus died and rose for you.

Because Jesus died and rose for you, your life today is now an all-encompassing yes.

Forever

This world is fading away, along with everything it craves.
But if you do the will of God, you will live forever.

1 JOHN 2:17 NLT

Forever is a beautiful word. When our reference point is God and His kingdom, everything takes on an eternal perspective. Life is filled with meaning and packed with purpose.

Everything that God is, He is eternally. He is love, and He loves you all the time. He is good, and He is good to you all the time. There are no ups and downs, highs and lows, or comes and goes with God. So you can sing and rejoice in the Lord forever, and forever His goodness and unfailing love will be yours.

What He was for you yesterday when He showed you mercy and grace, He will be for you today. The acceptance you knew when He lifted you out of your sins is the same acceptance that upholds you today. The arms that were once around you to give you assurance embrace you today. All the delights of His presence, all the joys of His face, all the gladness of His heart, rest upon you today.

Today Is Your Best Day Because...
God Is with You

Fear not, for I am with you; be not dismayed, for I am your God.
I will strengthen you, yes, I will help you, I will uphold you
with My righteous right hand.

Isaiah 41:10 NKJV

Because God is with you, He does not want you to fear or be dismayed. Because God is with you, He will strengthen you and help you and uphold you with His righteous right hand.

Whatever your fears may be today or whoever your enemies are, you have a Friend who sticks closer to you than a brother. Today is your best day because you do not walk through it alone, abandoned, or forsaken. God is with you and He can handle any situation you face, any foe you encounter, any problem you meet, or any conflict you confront. One plus God is definitely a majority! God's presence with you is the reason He gives you not to fear.

Remember, God has a firm hold upon you. God is not only with you today, but His mighty hand is holding on to you with every step you take.

Intercessory Prayer

Therefore He is also able to save to the uttermost those who come to God through Him, since He always lives to make intercession for them.

HEBREWS 7:25 NKJV

How rich you are when someone is praying for you. It has been said that the poorest person is the one who has no one praying for him. You will never have full knowledge of how many times someone has prayed for you, or how often God has prompted someone to pray for you when you were in need. Those prayers have impacted your life at many times and in many ways.

Today is your best day because prayer has made this day possible. I don't know how many people are praying for you today, but I am certain that at least one person is. As you seek to walk in the calling of a holy life, as you face temptation, as you seek the Father's will and His glory, someone is praying for you.

That person is Jesus Christ. He is your faithful Advocate and High Priest. He is the One who saves you to the uttermost, and His intercession for you is to the highest degree possible. He will always be interceding on your behalf.

God Meets Your Every Need

How blessed is God! And what a blessing he is! He's the Father of our Master, Jesus Christ, and takes us to the high places of blessing in him. Long before he laid down earth's foundations, he had us in mind, had settled on us as the focus of his love, to be made whole and holy by his love.

EPHESIANS 1:3–4 MSG

What are your deepest needs and desires? They are not entertainment, wealth, sports, scholastic achievement, popularity, power, or influence. Your greatest needs and desires are matters of your heart and spirit. They are the deepest things within you that cry out for purpose, fulfillment, intimacy, meaning, and love. They are the longings that God has placed within you and that only He can meet.

Your cries for belonging He alone can answer; your search for meaning He alone can fulfill; your thirst for fulfillment He alone can quench; your longing for intimacy He alone can satisfy. He has met your need for protection by being your Strong Tower and your Hiding Place. He has met your need for wholeness by being your Healer. He has met your need for peace by being your Shalom.

TODAY IS YOUR BEST DAY BECAUSE...

God Satisfies

*My God shall supply all your need
according to His riches in glory by Christ Jesus.*

PHILIPPIANS 4:19 NKJV

God, through His Son, has already satisfied your need for redemption, forgiveness, and reconciliation by being your Redeemer. He has met your need for righteousness by becoming your righteousness; He has met your need for security by holding you secure in His arms; He has met your need for companionship by being the God who is there.

He has met your need for guidance and direction by being your Shepherd and Guide. Your need for hope and comfort has been met by Him, for He is the God of all hope and comfort. And He has met your need for love by being the God who has loved you with an everlasting love.

Today as you long for living waters, remember that He invites the thirsty to drink; as you seek His presence, remember that He bids you to draw near; as you desire to know His heart, remember that you are the object of His love.

TODAY IS YOUR BEST DAY…

and the Future Will Be Even Better

Looking for the blessed hope and glorious appearing
of our great God and Savior Jesus Christ.

TITUS 2:13 NKJV

The world we live in is a very uncertain place. As people look to the future, their fears and concerns only deepen as they worry about what will happen and wonder how things will turn out.

As a believer in Jesus Christ your future outlook is an upward look. You have a hope and a future that is glorious. The Word of God has already declared to you what the future will be and how things will turn out in the end. You can live today in calmness of soul and peace of heart because the final outcome has already been determined by God. You are on the winning side. Jesus Christ will come for you with a shout, with the voice of the archangel, and with the trumpet of God. He will come triumphant, in power, and full of glory. He will establish His reign upon this earth and rule with a scepter of righteousness. His kingdom is an everlasting kingdom, and you will be a part of it all.

Today Is Your Best Day Because of...

Heaven

For God has reserved a priceless inheritance for his children.
It is kept in heaven for you, pure and undefiled,
beyond the reach of change and decay.

1 Peter 1:4 nlt

If you are alive on this earth when Jesus Christ returns, you will be caught up to be with Him forever. What a day that will be! If you were to die today, before the Lord returns, this would still be your best day. Your last day upon this earth will be your first day in heaven. The Bible tells us that to be "absent from the body" is "to be present with the Lord" (see 2 Corinthians 5:8 nkjv).

In heaven you will go from a temporary life to an eternal life, from a world of darkness to a place of everlasting light, from a life of walking by faith to a life of seeing Jesus face-to-face.

In heaven all your tears will be wiped away, all your sorrows will vanish from view, all your weaknesses will be swallowed up in His majesty, and all your suffering will give way to eternal shouts of joy. This is the hope all believers in Jesus have. This is the hope that makes every day your best day!

Ellie Claire™ Gift & Paper Corp.
Minneapolis, MN 55337
www.ellieclaire.com

Today Is Your Best Day
Promise Journal
© 2011 by Roy Lessin

ISBN 978-1-60936-239-3

Cover and interior design by David Carlson, Gearbox

Printed in China